1 MONTH OF
FREE
READING

at
www.ForgottenBooks.com

By purchasing this book you are eligible for one month membership to ForgottenBooks.com, giving you unlimited access to our entire collection of over 1,000,000 titles via our web site and mobile apps.

To claim your free month visit:

www.forgottenbooks.com/free919633

ISBN 978-0-266-98776-5
PIBN 10919633

For support please visit www.forgottenbooks.com

NATIONAL RECOVERY ADMINISTRATION

CODE OF FAIR COMPETITION

FOR THE

FERTILIZER INDUSTRY

AS APPROVED ON OCTOBER 31, 1933

BY

PRESIDENT ROOSEVELT

1. Executive Order
2. Letter of Transmittal
3. Code

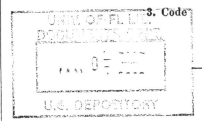

UNITED STATES
GOVERNMENT PRINTING OFFICE
WASHINGTON : 1933

DISTRICT OFFICES OF THE DEPARTMENT OF COMMERCE

Atlanta, Ga.: 504 Post Office Building.
Birmingham, Ala.: 257 Federal Building.
Boston, Mass.: 1801 Customhouse.
Buffalo, N.Y.: Chamber of Commerce Building.
Charleston, S.C.: Chamber of Commerce Building.
Chicago, Ill.: Suite 1706, 201 North Wells Street.
Cleveland, Ohio: Chamber of Commerce.
Dallas, Tex.: Chamber of Commerce Building.
Detroit, Mich.: 2213 First National Building.
Houston, Tex.: Chamber of Commerce Building.
Indianapolis, Ind.: Chamber of Commerce Building.
Jacksonville, Fla.: Chamber of Commerce Building.
Kansas City, Mo.: 1028 Baltimore Avenue.
Los Angeles, Calif: 1163 South Broadway.
Louisville, Ky.: 408 Federal Building.
Memphis, Tenn.: 229 Federal Building.
Minueapolis, Minn.: 213 Federal Building.
New Orleans, La.: Room 225-A, Customhouse.
New York, N.Y.: 734 Customhouse.
Norfolk, Va.: 406 East Plume Street.
Philadelphia, Pa.: 933 Commercial Trust Building.
Pittsburgh, Pa.: Chamber of Commerce Building.
Portland, Oreg.: 215 New Post Office Building.
St. Louis, Mo.: 506 Olive Street.
San Francisco, Calif.: 310 Customhouse.
Seattle, Wash.: 809 Federal Building.

EXECUTIVE ORDER

Code of Fair Competition for the Fertilizer Industry

An application having been duly made, pursuant to and in full compliance with the provisions of title I of the National Industrial Recovery Act, approved June 16, 1933, for my approval of a Code of Fair Competition for the Fertilizer Industry, and hearings having been held thereon and the Administrator having rendered his report containing an analysis of the said code of fair competition together with his recommendations and findings with respect thereto, and the Administrator having found that the said code of fair competition complies in all respects with the pertinent provisions of title I of said act and that the requirements of clauses (1) and (2) of subsection (a) of section 3 of the said act have been met:

NOW, THEREFORE, I, Franklin D. Roosevelt, President of the United States, pursuant to the authority vested in me by title I of the National Industry Recovery Act, approved June 16, 1933, and otherwise, do adopt and approve the report, recommendations, and findings of the Administrator and do order that the said code of fair competition be, and is hereby, approved.

FRANKLIN D. ROOSEVELT.

The White House,
        October 31, 1933.
Approval recommended:
    Hugh S. Johnson,
        Administrator.

(III)

The PRESIDENT,
    The White House, Washington, D.C.

SIR: This is a report of the hearing on the Code of Fair Competition for the Fertilizer Industry conducted in Washington on the 6th of September 1933 in accordance with the provisions of the National Industrial Recovery Act.

PROVISIONS OF THIS CODE AS TO HOURS AND WAGES

ARTICLE IV

SECTION 2. *Maximum Hours of Labor.*—a. No employee in the fertilizer industry shall be required or permitted to work more than 40 hours in any one week or eight hours in any one day except as follows:

1. Foremen, superintendents, managers, salesmen, chemists, and officials.

2. During the rush of the planting season the hours of labor may exceed the maximum above prescribed by eight hours a week, and in the case of skilled key men the hours of labor may exceed the maximum above prescribed by 20 hours in any week, but in no event shall employees be permitted to work more than an average of 40 hours a week over any consecutive four-months' period.

3. Office employees shall not be required or permitted to work more than an average of 40 hours a week in any four months' period.

4. Employees engaged in any continuous operation when other competent employees are readily available for such work shall not be required or permitted to work more than 40 hours in any one week, and in no case more than 48 hours in any one week.

5. Repair shop crews, engineers, electricians, and watching crews shall not be required or permitted to work more than 40 hours in any one week, with a tolerance of 10 percent, except in the case of emergency.

b. Overtime shall be paid at the rate of one and one third times the normal rate for all work in the excess of eight hours a day, except in the case of office employees.

c. Every employee in the fertilizer industry shall be entitled to one day of rest a week.

SECTION 3. *Minimum Rates of Pay.*—a. No employee in the fertilizer industry shall be paid less than the following: 35 cents an hour in the Northern area, 25 cents an hour in the Southern area, 35 cents an hour in the Midwestern area, 40 cents an hour in the Pacific Coast area, and 20 cents an hour in Puerto Rico.

b. The Northern area comprises Maine, New Hampshire, Vermont, Massachusetts, Connecticut, Rhode Island, New York, Pennsylvania, New Jersey, Maryland (except the Eastern Shore), Newcastle County of Delaware, District of Columbia, and West Virginia.

c. The Southern area comprises Kent and Sussex Counties of Delaware, the Eastern Shore of Maryland, Virginia, North Carolina, South Carolina, Georgia, Florida, Alabama, Mississippi, Arkansas, Louisiana, Oklahoma, Texas, and Tennessee.

d. The Midwestern area comprises Ohio, Illinois, Indiana, Kentucky, Missouri, Kansas, Nebraska, South Dakota, North Dakota, Colorado, New Mexico, Arizona, Wyoming, Montana, Michigan, Wisconsin Minnesota and Iowa.

e. The Pacific Coast area comprises Washington, Oregon, California, Idaho, Nevada, and Utah.

ECONOMIC EFFECT OF THE CODE

The Fertilizer Industry, as covered by the attached Code, is an industry whose activity is intimately connected with the income and purchasing power of the farmer. Since 1929 gross agricultural income has declined from $10,000,000,000 to a little over $4,000,000,000, and has been accompanied by a decline in annual fertilizer consumption from 8,000,000 tons to 4,000,000 tons.

Basically, this Code covers the mixers of fertilizer, some 600 in number, operating approximately 800 plants. Nearly three fourths of these plants are located in the one-crop sections of the South and Southeast producing fertilizer to be used in connection with the cotton and tobacco crops. In addition to the mixed fertilizer produced by these plants, certain unmixed substances, such as potash, nitrogen carriers and so forth, which may be used directly on the soil, are in competition with mixed fertilizer. A large proportion of such material is handled by the fertilizer mixing concerns, but some portion is marketed direct to dealers and consumers by the producers of such materials, and even by their importers. Importations of nitrate carriers, such as Chilean nitrate of soda, potash from Germany and superphosphate from Japan, have a serious effect on this industry and, to a certain extent, have contributed to the demoralization of the industry. For this reason the Code contains a great number of unfair trade practices which are to be prohibited, and covers not only the mixing of fertilizer and its immediate sale, but also covers (as far as sales to dealers and consumers are concerned) the distribution of the competing products.

It is believed that, for the ultimate good of the farmer, the control prescribed and permitted in this Code is essential. In view of these conditions, however, it is highly important that the Government representation on the operation of this Code exercise carefully its functions.

The fertilizer industry is one with extremely seasonal operation. Thirty-five percent of the annual production of this industry is moved in one month and 85% of it is moved in approximately three months of each year. This period is a period of farm activity. The product is bulky and the plants, as a whole, are located near the consumer—that is, in agricultural areas. The percentage of common labor reaches to more than 70% of the total labor employed and is of the farm labor type. It seems important, therefore, that scales of wages be not set up so high as to disrupt the agricultural situation in the vicinity of fertilizer factories.

The highest recorded employment in the fertilizer industry was reached in March 1929, when nearly 38,000 workers were employed. The average or more normal figure of 1928 was 33,000 employees. This had decreased in 1932 to only 21,000 employees. The above figures, of course, apply to the peak season, during which the greatest portion of fertilizer is being mixed and delivered.

The reduction in hours in this Code to an average of 40 for a four months' period, with overtime for all work in excess of eight hours per day, should increase the number of employees in the peak season to about 27,500 workers at the same scale of purchasing by agriculture as now exists. It is to be presumed, however, that betterment in prices of the products of agriculture will permit the purchase of increased quantities of fertilizer.

The wages established in this Code are such as to increase nearly 100% of the employees in the Southern area, and 90% of the employees in the Northern and Western areas. It will increase the wages of nearly 78% of the employees in the Pacific Coast area. The average wage in the Southern area in 1923 was 13.7 cents per hour, whereas the Code provides a minimum wage of 25 cents per hour. The average wage for the spring of 1923 in the Northern Area was 26.5 cents per hour, while the Code provides 35 cents per hour. It will be seen, therefore, that not only will this Code increase employment materially, but will raise very greatly the rate of pay throughout the entire United States.

While the absolute wage rates provided by the Code still are not high, it is believed that this industry with its close interlock with agriculture can be affected only adversely if higher minimum wages are required.

FINDINGS

The Administrator finds that (a) The Code as recommended complies in all respects with the pertinent provisions of Title I of the Act, including, without limitation, subsection (a) of Section 7 and subsection (b) of Section 10 thereof; and that

(b) The applicant group imposes no inequitable restrictions on admission to membership therein and is truly representative of the Fertilizer Industry; and that

(c) The Code as recommended is not designed to promote monopolies or to eliminate or oppress small enterprises and will not operate to discriminate against them, and will tend to effectuate the policy of Title I of the National Industrial Recovery Act.

It is recommended, therefore, that this Code be immediately adopted.

Respectfully,

HUGH S. JOHNSON,
Administrator.

CODE OF FAIR COMPETITION FOR THE FERTILIZER INDUSTRY

The following provisions shall constitute the Code of Fair Competition for the fertilizer industry under the National Industrial Recovery Act:

ARTICLE I—PURPOSE

It is the purpose of this Code to aid in eliminating from the fertilizer industry destructive and unfair methods of competition, waste, and improper practices, to place the industry upon a sounder basis and better enable it to serve labor and agriculture by bringing about higher wages, shorter working hours, better living conditions for employees, fair prices, and high-quality products for the farmer, and reasonable profit to the producers of fertilizer and to the industry generally.

ARTICLE II—DEFINITIONS

SECTION 1. a. The term " fertilizer industry " as used herein includes the importation, production, and/or distribution of mixed fertilizer, superphosphate, and/or other fertilizer materials. This Code does *not* cover sulphuric acid, nor does it cover dealers. This Code does *not* cover the production of potash, phosphate rock, and/or nitrogen carriers, nor does it cover their distribution to producers and to persons other than dealers or consumers. This Code *does* cover the sale and distribution of potash, phosphate rock, and/or nitrogen carriers to dealers and/or consumers, whether made directly or through agents: Provided, however, that such sale and distribution by producers of such materials shall be exempted from the provisions of Article V, Production and New Capacity; Article VI, Price Provisions, Section 1, Sales Below Cost Prohibited; and Sections 1, 2, 4, 5, and 6 of Article VII, Marketing Provisions, and shall also be exempted from the requirements of Article IX, Reports and Statistics, to the extent that producers of such materials shall not be required thereunder to submit any reports or information concerning their costs of production, wages, hours of labor, other conditions of labor, or prices to others than dealers or consumers.

b. In the event that any producer or importer of potash, phosphate rock, or nitrogen carriers makes no sale of mixed fertilizer, superphosphate, or other fertilizer material to dealers and/or consumers, none of the provisions of this Code shall apply to such producer or importer. Provided, further, that if and when the producers and/or importers of potash shall have filed a Code of Fair Competition covering the sale and distribution of potash to dealers and/or consumers, which Code shall contain provisions the same as

Article VI, Section 2, Open-Price Schedules; Article VII, Section 3, Distribution Through Cooperative Associations, Section 7, Methods of Quoting Prices, Methods of Distribution, and Methods of Delivery, Section 8, Exemptions from Marketing Provisions, and all Sections of Article VIII, Unfair Practices Prohibited, in the form as approved by the President herein, and such Code with such provisions shall have been approved by the President and become effective, such sale and distribution of potash shall be exempted entirely from this Code. Similarly, if and when the producers and/or importers of phosphate rock and/or nitrogen carriers shall have filed a Code of Fair Competition covering the sale and distribution of phosphate rock and/or nitrogen carriers to dealers and/or consumers, which Code shall contain the provisions just recited, and such Code with such provisions shall have been approved by the President and become effective, such sale and distribution of phosphate rock and/or nitrogen carriers shall be exempted entirely from this Code.

SEC. 2. The term "employee" as used herein includes any person engaged in any phase of the industry in any capacity in the nature of employee, irrespective of the method of payment of his compensation.

SEC. 3. The term "employer" as used herein includes anyone for whose benefit such an employee is so engaged.

SEC. 4. The term "mixed fertilizer" means any combination or mixture of fertilizer materials, designed and fit for use in inducing increased crop yields or plant growth when applied to the soil.

SEC. 5. The term "fertilizer material" means any substance which is used with another substance in the manufacture of mixed fertilizers, or for direct application to the soil, principally as a source of plant food, except unmanipulated manures of domestic origin.

SEC. 6. The term "superphosphate" means the product resulting from mixing rock phosphate and sulphuric acid and/or phosphoric acid.

SEC. 7. The term "grade" as applied to mixed fertilizer, shall represent the minimum guarantee of its plant food expressed in terms of nitrogen, available phosphoric acid, and water soluble potash, and such other substances as may be guaranteed.

SEC. 8. The term "dealer" means any person, other than a producer, engaged in the business of buying mixed fertilizer, superphosphate, and/or other fertilizer material for the purpose of selling at a profit. One buying for his own use, or principally for his own use and that of his tenants, shall not be deemed to be a dealer. A group of unincorporated consumer buyers acting collectively or through an individual for the purpose of contracting for a joint order is not a dealer.

SEC. 9. The term "agent" means any person engaged in the business of distributing mixed fertilizer, superphosphate, and/or other fertilizer materials for a fixed compensation as provided in the producer's price list, and who guarantees the whole and complete performance of the terms of his contract with the producer.

SEC. 10. The term "Fertilizer Recovery Committee" means the Committee created in accordance with Article III of this Code.

Sec. 11. The term "zone" means a geographical division of the United States established under Article III of this Code.

Sec. 12. The term "producer" means any member of the industry engaged in the business of preparing, mixing, manufacturing, or importing mixed fertilizer, superphosphate, and/or other fertilizer material for sale.

ARTICLE III—ADMINISTRATION

Section 1. To effectuate further the policies of the Act, a Fertilizer Recovery Committee is hereby designated to cooperate with the Administrator as a Planning and Fair Practice Agency for the fertilizer industry. This Committee, constituting the Code Authority, shall consist of not less than twelve representatives of the fertilizer industry selected by a fair method of selection to be approved by the Administrator. Three members without vote may be appointed by the President of the United States.

Sec. 2. The Code Authority is hereby empowered to collect from the industry such statistical information as, in the opinion of the Administrator, may be necessary to effectuate Title I of the National Industrial Recovery Act and this Code. In addition to such information there shall be furnished to the Federal Trade Commission, for the use of the President of the United States, such information as the Federal Trade Commission or the President may deem necessary for the purposes recited in Section 3 (a) of the National Industrial Recovery Act. Such information may include wages, hours of labor, prices, production, stocks, orders, shipments, production capacity, and costs. Any or all information furnished to the Federal Trade Commission by any member of the industry shall be subject to checking by said Commission for the purpose of verification by an examination of the books and accounts and records of such member.

Sec. 3. In carrying out its functions, said Committee, subject to the approval of the Administrator, is authorized to divide the United States into appropriate trade zones based on such geographical, trade, and/or other conditions as shall best serve the purposes of this Code, and to change such zones from time to time as may be found necessary.

Sec. 4. The Code Authority may delegate or appoint individuals and subcommittees in carrying out its administrative work, with such of its power or powers as may from time to time be conferred by the Code Authority upon said individuals or subcommittees, responsibility, however, to remain with the Code Authority.

Sec. 5. The Code Authority shall appoint, from its own membership, an Administrative Committee of eight members. Said Committee shall exercise such authority as may have been delegated to it by the Code Authority except that the Administrative Committee shall not make recommendations for the amendment of this Code unless recommendations for such amendments have been approved in writing by two thirds of the members of the Code Authority. The Administrative Committee shall serve as the executive agency of the Fertilizer Recovery Committee, which constitutes the Code Authority.

ARTICLE IV—LABOR PROVISIONS

SECTION 1. *Collective Bargaining.*—Pursuant to Section 7 (a) of the National Industrial Recovery Act, the following provisions are hereby embodied in and prescribed as part of this Code:

a. That employees shall have the right to organize and bargain collectively through representatives of their own choosing, and shall be free from the interference, restraint, or coercion of employers of labor, or their agents, in the designation of such representatives or in self-organization or m other concerted activities for the purpose of collective bargaining or other mutual aid or protection.

b. That no employee and no one seeking employment shall be required as a condition of employment to join any company union or to refrain from joining, organizing, or assisting a labor organization of his own choosing.

c. That employers shall comply with the maximum hours of labor, minimum rates of pay, and other conditions of employment, approved or prescribed by the President.

SEC. 2. *Maximum Hours of Labor.*—a. No employee in the fertilizer industry shall be required or permitted to work more than 40 hours in any one week or eight hours in any one day except as follows:

1. Foremen, superintendents, managers, salesmen, chemists, and officials.

2. During the rush of the planting season the hours of labor may exceed the maximum above prescribed by eight hours a week, and in the case of skilled key men the hours of labor may exceed the maximum above prescribed by 20 hours in any week, but in no event shall employees be permitted to work more than an average of 40 hours a week over any consecutive four-months' period.

3. Office employees shall not be required or permitted to work more than an average of 40 hours a week in any four-months' period.

4. Employees engaged in any continuous operation when other competent employees are readily available for such work shall not be required or permitted to work more than 40 hours in any one week, and in no case more than 48 hours in any one week.

5· Repair shop crews, engineers, electricians, and watching crews shall not be required or permitted to work more than 40 hours in any one week, with a tolerance of 10 per cent, except in the case of emergency.

b. Overtime shall be paid at the rate of one and one third times the normal rate for all work in the excess of eight hours a day, except in the case of office employees.

c. Every employee in the fertilizer industry shall be entitled to one day of rest a week.

SEC. 3. *Minimum Rates of Pay.*—a. No employee in the fertilizer industry shall be paid less than the following: 35 cents an hour in the Northern area, 25 cents an hour in the Southern area, 35 cents an hour in the Midwestern area, 40 cents an hour in the Pacific Coast area, and 20 cents an hour in Puerto Rico.

b. The Northern area comprises Maine, New Hampshire, Vermont, Massachusetts, Connecticut, Rhode Island, New York, Pennsylvania, New Jersey, Maryland (except the Eastern Shore), New Castle County of Delaware, District of Columbia, and West Virginia.

c. The Southern area comprises Kent and Sussex Counties of Delaware, the Eastern Shore of Maryland, Virginia, North Carolina, South Carolina, Georgia, Florida, Alabama, Mississippi, Arkansas, Louisiana, Oklahoma, Texas, and Tennessee.

d. The Midwestern area comprises Ohio, Illinois, Indiana, Kentucky, Missouri, Kansas, Nebraska, South Dakota, North Dakota, Colorado, New Mexico, Arizona, Wyoming, Montana, Michigan, Wisconsin, Minnesota, and Iowa.

e. The Pacific Coast area comprises Washington, Oregon, California, Idaho, Nevada, and Utah.

SEC. 4. *Child Labor Prohibited.*—No employee under the age of 16 years shall be employed in the fertilizer industry.

SEC. 5. *Reclassification of Functions Prohibited.*—There shall be no evasion of this Code by reclassification of the function of employees. An employee shall not be included in any of the exceptions set forth above unless the identical functions were identically classified on June 15, 1933.

ARTICLE V—PRODUCTION AND NEW CAPACITY

Should it at any time appear that the policy of Title I of the National Industrial Recovery Act will not be effectuated in the industry because of overproduction, the Fertilizer Recovery Committee may submit to the Administrator recommendations for amendments to this Code or for such other action as may be appropriate.

ARTICLE VI—PRICE PROVISIONS

SECTION 1. *Sales Below Cost Prohibited.*—The sale or offer for sale by any producer of mixed fertilizer, superphosphate, and/or other fertilizer material at a price below his cost except to meet existing competition is hereby prohibited. The term " cost " as used herein means the cost determined in accordance with uniform methods of accounting which shall be prescribed hereunder by the Fertilizer Recovery Committee with the approval of the National Recovery Administration. Such cost shall properly define the differences in factory, manufacturing, and mixing costs, and costs of distributing the product to producers, dealers, agents, and consumers, and such differences in cost shall be reflected in the sales price to each of these classifications.

SEC. 2. *Open Price Schedules.*—a. Within five days after this Code becomes effective each producer shall file with the Secretary of The National Fertilizer·Association:

1. A statement showing in what zones said producer intends to sell mixed fertilizer, superphosphate, and/or other fertilizer material;

2. A schedule by zones of the prices than in effect or to be charged for all grades or kinds of mixed fertilizer, superphosphate, and/or other fertilizer material sold or offered for sale to dealers, agents, or consumers by such producer, together with the terms and conditions applicable; thereto; and,

3. Shall mail or deliver true copies of such schedule to his competitors in the zones where such producer does business.

b. If the original schedule so filed by any producer represents any change in his then existing prices, terms, or conditions, it shall not become effective until the expiration of 48 hours after it is filed. After the original schedule is filed, no mixed fertilizer, superphosphate, and/or other fertilizer material shall be sold or offered for sale by such producer at a price or on terms or conditions other than as specified in said schedule or in a new schedule that has become effective pursuant to the provisions of this Section.

c. No new schedule advancing or reducing any price or changing the terms or conditions shall be deemed to have become effective hereunder until a date and hour ten days after it has been filed with the Secretary of The National Fertilizer Association and unless simultaneously with such filing true copies thereof have been mailed or delivered by such producer to other producers in the zones where the producer who files the schedule is doing business, except that any such schedule filed to meet a new or changed schedule filed by a competitor may become effective on the same date and hour that the competitor's schedule becomes effective if a copy thereof is filed with the Secretary of The National Fertilizer Association and copies have been mailed or delivered to other producers in the same zones at least 48 hours before such effective date and hour. Any original, new, or changed schedule when filed shall be open to inspection by any producer.

d. Upon receipt from any producer of any original or new schedule representing a change in prices, terms, or conditions, the Secretary of The National Fertilizer Association shall immediately mail to such producer and to other producers in the zones to which such schedule relates a notice of the date and hour of filing of such schedule and when it becomes effective.

e. There shall be attached to each schedule filed hereunder a statement specifying the changes made therein from the last preceding schedule. The original schedule of each producer filed hereunder shall be numbered " one " and all subsequent schedules or changes in schedules shall be numbered serially in accordance with a uniform plan of numbering prescribed by The National Fertilizer Association.

ARTICLE VII—MARKETING PROVISIONS

SECTION 1. *Reduction in Number of Grades of Mixed Fertilizer.*— In order to eliminate waste and reduce the cost of manufacture, bearing in mind the economic interest of the farmer, a list of grades suitable to meet the agricultural needs of each State or of each zone, as the case may be, may be established by the producers in such zone or State, acting through a zone committee, in cooperation with agronomists and other Federal and State agricultural officials, subject to the approval of the National Recovery Administration. After such grades have been established for such State or zone, the sale or offer for sale therein of mixed fertilizer not conforming to the grades so established shall be considered an unfair trade practice, provided that the sale of special formulas or special ingredients in standard formulas may be made to satisfy bona fide orders from customers if adequate additional charge is made for mixing costs as determined for the particular plant under the uniform accounting methods prescribed in Article VI plus the extra cost of special materials used; and provided that this shall not prevent any producer from selling or offering for sale two extra grades for lawns and gardens in various-sized packages not to exceed 100 pounds a package.

SEC. 2. *Sales Through Commission Traveling Salesmen Prohibited.*—No traveling salesman shall be employed on a commission basis for the sale of mixed fertilizer, superphosphate, and/or other fertilizer material. Such sales shall be made only through regular, legitimate, salaried salesmen working under the control of the producer. This Section shall not apply to the State of Florida.

SEC. 3. *Distribution Through Cooperative Associations.*—a. Any arrangement upon sale, consignment, or agency basis between producers and regularly incorporated farmers' organizations engaged in the various activities common to such organizations and principally engaged in a bona fide wholesale business or their divisions or departments granting special rates, commissions, or concessions, or the division of profits, may be continued, entered into, and performed, provided that such sales are not below the producer's price as provided in Article VI, Section 1 of this Code, and that it shall be obligatory upon such cooperative organizations to maintain the producer's schedule of prices to their dealers and consumers in the areas covered.

b. No provisions of this Code shall be interpreted as preventing farmers' cooperative corporations from paying patronage dividends as authorized by law.

SEC. 4.—*Sales to Dealer and Consumer Through Brokers Prohibited.*—The sale by the producer of mixed fertilizer and/or bagged superphosphate to the dealer or consumer through brokers is hereby prohibited.

SEC. 5. *Uniform Contracts.*—Subject to the approval of the National Recovery Administration, the Fertilizer Recovery Committee is authorized to prepare and prescribe, according to appropriate zones established by it, uniform forms of contracts for use in the sale by producers of mixed fertilizer, superphosphate, and/or other fertilizer material. After such forms have been so prescribed for any zone as to any type of transaction the sale by any producer in such zone of mixed fertilizer, superphosphate, and/or other fertilizer material under any form of contract for such type of transaction other than the form so prescribed is hereby prohibited.

SEC. 6. *Investigation of Imports.*—The Fertilizer Recovery Committee is authorized to investigate or cause to be investigated and to report to the National Recovery Administration in behalf of the fertilizer industry the facts as to the importation into the United States and Puerto Rico of mixed fertilizer, superphosphate, and/or other fertilizer material in substantial quantities or increasing ratio to domestic production and on such terms or under such conditions as to render ineffective or seriously to endanger the maintenance of this Code.

SEC. 7. *Methods of Quoting Prices, Methods of Distribution, and Methods of Delivery.*—The producers in each zone, acting in accordance with procedure established by the Fertilizer Recovery Committee and subject to its approval, are authorized to prepare uniform rules, not inconsistent with any provision in this Code, governing the methods of quoting prices, methods of distribution, and methods of delivery, including trucking allowances, to be used in the sale of mixed fertilizer, superphosphate, and/or other fertilizer material in such zone or subdivision thereof. Such rules, when so prepared and approved by the Fertilizer Recovery Committee, shall be submitted to the National Recovery Administration, and when approved by it shall be binding upon all producers selling said products in such zone or subdivision thereof.

SEC. 8. *Exemptions from Marketing Provisions.*—a. In view of the peculiar marketing conditions existing in zone 11a, it is exempted from Section 2 of Article VII, Marketing Provisions, of this Code.

b. The States of Idaho, Utah, Montana, Colorado, Wyoming, and Nebraska are exempt from all regulatory rules pertaining to sales.

ARTICLE VIII—UNFAIR PRACTICES PROHIBITED

The following shall be deemed to be unfair competition within the meaning of the National Industrial Recovery Act and are hereby prohibited:

SECTION 1. The defamation of a competitor by falsely imputing to such competitor dishonorable conduct, inability to perform contracts, questionable credit standing, or by other false representations, or the false disparagement of the grade or quality of his goods, with the tendency and capacity to mislead or deceive purchasers or prospective purchasers.

SEC. 2. The payment or allowance, except as required by law, of rebates, refunds, or unearned commissions or discounts, or of claims known to be false or unjustified, whether in the form of money or otherwise, or extending to certain purchasers special services or privileges not extended to all purchasers under like terms and conditions.

SEC. 3. The payment to any person who is not a dealer or agent, as defined herein, in connection with the sale of any mixed fertilizer, superphosphate, and/or other fertilizer material of any compensation or allowance to which a dealer or agent is entitled.

SEC. 4. Withholding from or inserting in any invoice a statement which makes the invoice false regarding the whole or any part of the transaction represented on the face thereof.

SEC. 5. Providing transportation without adequate charge for it, or reimbursing, the dealer, agent, purchaser, or consignee for the costs of transportation if reimbursement is not provided for in the producer's price list.

SEC 6. The operation or use by a producer of any warehouse owned or controlled by such producer, or of any warehouse or warehouse space leased by him for the storage of mixed fertilizer, superphosphate, and/or other fertilizer material, in such way or under such circumstances as to result in the granting of rebates, or special allowances from the contract price of any mixed fertilizer, superphosphate, and/or other fertilizer material sold or offered for sale by such producer, or the making by any producer in connection with the sale of mixed fertilizer, superphosphate, and/or other fertilizer material of an allowance for warehousing not included in his price schedule.

SEC. 7. Selling or consigning chemicals and materials with special concessions or at reduced prices, given to induce the purchase of mixed fertilizer, superphosphate, and/or other fertilizer material.

SEC. 8. Failure to enforce in good faith the terms of contracts previously made for the sale of mixed fertilizer, superphosphate, and/or other fertilizer material, as for example:

a. Selling on terms that require the payment of sight draft on presentation of bill of lading (S.D.B.L.) and then waiving the obligation to pay cash before documents or goods are delivered, thus deferring the payment of the cash to some future date.

b. Selling and delivering goods on time, consignment, or open bill of lading terms on S.D.B.L. price, or waiving earned interest.

SEC. 9. Furnishing special containers, preparing special formulas for individual buyers or consignees, or using special ingredients in standard formulas, without adequate charge for the cost of such containers, formulas, or special ingredients, as an inducement to the making of a contract and/or sale.

SEC. 10. Making special allowance to buyers or consignees under the guise of advertising expense, or giving any other form of gratuity.

SEC. 11. Adopting selling methods that promote secret rebates and concessions, such as:

a. Employing a buyer or consignee or his agent or anyone employed by or connected with a buyer or consignee with the purpose, design, and effect of influencing the business of such customer.

b. Carrying on books by seller or consignee as delinquent balances due by solvent customer with no intention of requiring ultimate payment.

SEC. 12. Enabling the purchaser or consignee to obtain mixed fertilizer, superphosphate, and/or other fertilizer material apparently on cash terms, but in fact on credit extended to him by or through the producer, as, for example:

a. A transaction covered by a sight draft and bill of lading under which the purchaser or consignee is made to appear as honoring documents upon presentation by payment with his own funds, when in fact the cash involved was obtained in whole or in part upon a negotiable instrument (usually discounted at a bank) bearing the endorsement of the producer; or

b. A transaction by which the producer, although he does not actually endorse the obligation, renders himself legally or morally responsible for its payment if the purchaser or consignee shall fail to meet his obligation to the bank at maturity.

SEC. 13. Refunding to the buyer or consignee, either directly or indirectly, any part of the purchase price on account of goods accepted and/or settled for by the buyer or consignee under the terms of the contract. This practice is commonly referred to as " retroactive settlement."

SEC. 14. The guaranteeing of prices against decline to dealers, agents, or consumers.

SEC. 15. Inducing the breach of any contract for the sale of mixed fertilizer, superphosphate, and/or other fertilizer material by offering a lower price to the purchaser under such contract, or by any other means.

Sec. 16. The false marking or branding of any product of the industry which has the tendency to mislead or deceive customers or prospective customers as to the grade, quality, quantity, substance, character, nature, origin, size, finish, or preparation.

Sec. 17. The making or causing or permitting to be made or published of any false, untrue, or deceptive statement by way of advertisement or otherwise concerning the grade, quality, quantity, substance, character, nature, origin, size, or preparation of any product of the industry having the tendency and capacity to mislead or deceive purchasers or prospective purchasers.

Sec. 18. Furnishing of mixed fertilizer, superphosphate, and/or other fertilizer material by a producer to any consumer with the understanding that payment therefor shall be made by turning over to such producer a quantity, fixed in advance and without reference to the market price, of the crop produced by the use of such fertilizer.

Article IX—Reports and Statistics

Section 1. The Fertilizer Recovery Committee is authorized to prescribe, subject to the approval of the Administrator, regulations requiring the submission by producers at such reasonable times as it may designate, of reports containing information necessary for the administration and enforcement of this Code, including wages, hours of labor, other conditions of labor, prices, marketing practices, and such other items as may be required. Such reports shall be submitted only to the executive officer of The National Fertilizer Association. Except as otherwise provided in this Code, all reports submitted hereunder shall be treated as confidential and shall be open to inspection only by the persons employed by the Fertilizer Recovery Committee to administer this Code and by the authorized officials of the National Recovery Administration.

Article X—General Provisions

Section 1. No provision in this Code shall be interpreted or applied in such a manner as to:
    a. Promote monopolies or monopolistic practices;
    b. Permit or encourage unfair competition;
    c. Eliminate or oppress small enterprises; or
    d. Discriminate against small enterprises.

Sec. 2. This Code and all the provisions thereof are expressly made subject to the right of the President, in accordance with the provision of Subsection (b) of Section 10 of the National Industrial Recovery Act, from time to time to cancel or modify any order, approval, license, rule, or regulation issued under Title I of said Act, and specifically, but without limitation, to the right of the President to cancel or modify his approval of this Code or any conditions imposed by him upon his approval thereof.

Sec. 3. Nothing in this Code shall be deemed to constitute the participants therein partners for any purpose.

SEC. 4. Within each State, members of the industry shall comply with any laws of such State imposing more stringent requirements, regulating the age of employees, wages, hours of work, or health, fire, general working conditions, or standards of commodity.

ARTICLE XI—FEES AND EXPENSES

Each producer subject to the jurisdiction of this Code and accepting the benefits of the activities of the Code Authority hereunder, shall pay to the Code Authority his proportionate share of the amounts necessary to pay the cost of assembling, analyzing, and publication of such reports and data, and of the maintenance of the said Code Authority and its activities, as the Code Authority, with the approval of the Administrator, may prescribe.

ARTICLE XII—AMENDMENTS

The right is hereby reserved to alter, amend, or supplement this Code at any time by a majority vote of the Fertilizer Recovery Committee, subject to the approval of the President of the United States.

ARTICLE XIII—EFFECTIVE DATE

This Code shall become effective on the tenth day after its approval by the President of the United States and shall terminate on June 16, 1935, or sooner if the President shall by proclamation or the Congress shall by joint resolution declare that the emergency recognized by Section 1 of the National Industrial Recovery Act has ended.

SCHEDULE A

Zone No. 1:
Maine
New Hampshire
Vermont
Massachusetts
Rhode Island
Connecticut

Zone No. 2:
New York
Pennsylvania
New Jersey

Zone No. 3:
Maryland
Delaware
District of Columbia
Virginia north of James River including Accomac and Northampton counties
West Virginia (B. & O. Section)

Zone No. 4:
Virginia south of James River including Richmond
West Virginia (C. & O. Section)
North Carolina

Zone No. 5: South Carolina

Zone No. 6:
Georgia
Florida starting with the eastern boundaries of Columbia, Suwanee, Lafayette, and Taylor counties and extending west to the Apalachicola River

Zone No. 7: Florida east and south of Suwanee, Columbia, Lafayette, and Taylor counties

Zone No. 8:
Tennessee
Alabama
Mississippi
Florida west of the Apalachicola River
Louisiana east of the Mississippi River

Zone No. 9:
Arkansas
Louisiana west of Mississippi River
Texas
Oklahoma
New Mexico

Zone No. 10:
Michigan
Ohio
Indiana
Kentucky
Illinois
Wisconsin
Minnesota
Iowa
Missouri
North Dakota
South Dakota
Nebraska
Kansas
Montana
Wyoming
Colorado

Zone No. 11a:
California
Nevada
Utah
Arizona

Zone No. 11b:
Washington
Oregon
Idaho

Zone No. 11c: Hawaii

Zone No. 12: Puerto Rico

SCHEDULE B

14

Zone No. 10

L. W. Rowell, Swift & Co. Chicago, Ill.

Zone No. 11a

Weller Noble, The Pacific Guano & Fertilizer Co., Berkeley, Calif.

Zone No. 11b

George R. Clapp, Swift & Co., North Portland, Oregon

ADMINISTRATIVE COMMITTEE

John J. Watson	C. T. Melvin
Charles J. Brand	Oscar F. Smith
Horace Bowker	A. D. Strobhar
B. H. Brewster, Jr.	W. E. Valliant

O

CPSIA information can be obtained
at www.ICGtesting.com
Printed in the USA
BVHW051902051118

532208BV00025B/5188/P